Around the World
Games

Margaret Hall

Heinemann
LIBRARY

www.heinemann.co.uk/library
Visit our website to find out more information about **Heinemann Library** books.

To order:
 Phone +44 (0)1865 888066

Send a fax to +44 (0)1865 314091

Visit the Heinemann Bookshop at www.heinemann.co.uk/library to browse our catalogue and order online.

First published in Great Britain by Heinemann Library, Halley Court, Jordan Hill, Oxford OX2 8EJ, a division of Reed Educational and Professional Publishing Ltd. Heinemann is a registered trademark of Reed Educational and Professional Publishing Ltd.

OXFORD MELBOURNE AUCKLAND JOHANNESBURG BLANTYRE
GABORONE IBADAN PORTSMOUTH NH (USA) CHICAGO

Designed by Lisa Buckley
Originated by Dot Gradations
Printed in Hong Kong/China

ISBN 0431 15131 8 (hardback)   ISBN 0431 15136 9 (paperback)
06 05 04 03 02   07 06 05 04 03 02
10 9 8 7 6 5 4 3 2   10 9 8 7 6 5 4 3 2 1

British Library Cataloguing in Publication Data

Hall, Margaret
    Games. – (Around the world)
    1. Games – Juvenile Literature
    I. Title
    394.2'6

Acknowledgements

The publishers would like to thank the following for permission to reproduce photographs: Title page, p.18 Momatiuk Eastcott/The Image Works; p.4 Tmongkol-Unep-Still Pictures/Peter Arnold, Inc.; pp.5, 6 © Dinodia; p.7 Jeff Persons-Stock,Boston Inc./PictureQuest; p.8 Richard T. Nowitz/Corbis; pp.9, 12, 15, 21 © Cathy Melloan; p.10 Keren Su/Corbis; p.11 Topham/The Image Works; p.13 Patrick War/Corbis; p.14 © Victor Englebert; p.16 Jack Fields/Corbis; p.17 L. Goodsmith/The Image Works; p.19 B. Gibbs/TRIP; p.20 © Wolfgang Kaehler; p.22 Jacksonville Journal Courier/The Image Works; p.23 Deborah Harse/The Image Works; p.24 Still Pictures/Peter Arnold, Inc.; p.25 Sean Sprague/Panos Pictures; p.26 Joe Viesti-The Viesti Collection; p.27 Haga Library Inc.; p.28 Paul A. Souders/Corbis; p.29 Lauren Goodsmith/The Image Works.

Cover photograph reproduced with permission of Still Pictures/Peter Arnold.

Every effort has been made to contact copyright holders of any material reproduced in this book. Any omissions will be rectified in subsequent printings if notice is given to the publishers.

Contents

Some words are shown in bold, **like this.** You can find out what they mean by looking in the glossary.

Games around the world

People all around the world like to play games. They play games indoors and outdoors. They play with friends and by themselves.

Some games are only played in certain parts of the world. Others are played almost everywhere. A game might be played a bit differently from country to country.

Playing by the rules

Most games have **rules** that players should
follow. Some games do not have many
rules. These games are easy to learn and
easy to play.

Other games have many rules. It takes a long time to learn to play them. People may **practise** for years to become good at these games.

Playground games

Children everywhere play games like tag, ring-a-ring-a-roses, and hide-and-seek. These games have been played in the same way for hundreds of years.

Many playground games are the same no matter where they are played. The name of a game may change, but the **rules** are often alike.

Ball games

People play many games by throwing, rolling, kicking and hitting balls. Balls can be made of wood, rubber, leather, plastic or even paper.

People can play ball games like catch in pairs. They also play ball games with groups of people split into **teams**.

Running and chasing games

Long ago, people ran to get places quickly or to escape from danger. They also chased wild animals to use for food. Children played games to help them learn these **skills**.

Children still play running and chasing games today. They have races of many different kinds. They also chase each other just for fun.

Games with sticks and stones

People often use **resources** they find nearby to make **playing pieces** for games. That is why games like **mancala** were first played with small stones.

Games are still played with things found nearby. However, many games now use specially made playing pieces instead of sticks and stones.

Jumping games

Jumping games are easy to set up and easy to play. Hopscotch is a game that you can play alone or with a group of friends.

Children play all kinds of jumping games. They jump over rocks and ropes. Sometimes they even jump over each other!

String and rope games

Many people play games with string. They may tell stories about their **culture** as they move the strings. The same stories have been told like this for hundreds of years.

Tug-of-war is a rope game that is played in many places. The winner is the **team** that pulls the hardest. Skipping is another popular rope game.

Marble games

Many children like to play marbles. Most marbles are glass. They also can be made from stone, metal or clay. Some children play marbles with peas, beans or nuts!

Some marbles have special names. These names may be different in different parts of the world. Each kind of marble has its own use in a game.

Circle and hoop games

Some games are played in a circle. In one game, players pass something around. In another game, one player runs outside the circle trying to catch someone else.

In many parts of the world, children have fun rolling hoops over the ground. Sometimes they use sticks to push the hoops along.

Board games

Some games are played on a **game board**.
The board may be made from wood, paper
or stone. Often, the ground is used as
a board.

Many of the world's oldest games are board games. Some boards look almost the same today as they did when the games were first played hundreds of years ago.

Party and festival games

People often play games just because they are fun. They may also play games when it is time to **celebrate** at a party or **festival**.

Many festival games may have started as part of a **ceremony**. Games can be a good way to take part in the **culture** of a place.

More games

People play many kinds of games. They play with objects, numbers and words. They run, skip and jump. They throw, catch and spin things.

All around the world, people have favourite games. They may play alone or with friends. Everyone plays for the same reason. They want to have fun.

Photo list

Glossary

bamboo woody grass with a hollow stem

celebrate have a party or do something special

ceremony special words and actions that are used on important days

culture things that a group of people does and believes in

festival time of celebration, usually with special events

game board small area with markings for playing a game

mancala board game played with stones or glass pieces

playing piece something used to play a game

practise do something over and over to get better at it

religion what a person believes about God

resource things that people can use

rule how something should be done or how people should act

skill something people need to know or be able to do

team group of people playing together, usually against another team

More books to read

Games around the world, Dorling Kindersley, 2000

Playground games by Sallie Purkis, Longman, 1995

Time to play: children's games around the world by Emery Bernhard, Dutton, 1999

Toys and games by Godfrey Hall, Hodder Wayland, 1999

Index

Titles in the *Around the World* series include:

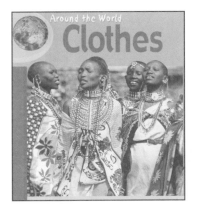

Hardback   0 431 15120 2

Hardback   0 431 15130 X

Hardback   0 431 15121 0

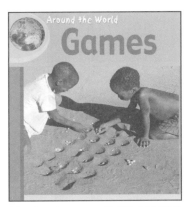

Hardback   0 431 15131 8

Hardback   0 431 15122 9

Hardback   0 431 15132 6

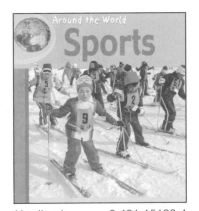

Hardback   0 431 15133 4

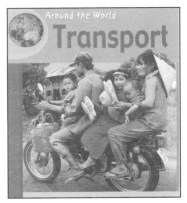

Hardback   0 431 15123 7

Find out about the other titles in this series on our website www.heinemann.co.uk/library